why Terry the Tree needed its mother?

Author

M Borhan

From

Big 6 Publishing

Trees play a crucial role in maintaining the balance and health of our natural environment. They contribute to biodiversity by providing habitats for countless species of plants, animals, and insects. Additionally, trees help to regulate the climate by absorbing carbon dioxide from the atmosphere and releasing oxygen through the process of photosynthesis. This process not only reduces greenhouse gas levels but also helps to mitigate the effects of climate change.

Moreover, trees play a vital role in soil conservation by preventing erosion and promoting soil health through their root systems. They also act as natural filters, purifying air and water by trapping pollutants and impurities. Furthermore, trees provide numerous economic and social benefits, including timber for construction, fuelwood, and various non-timber forest products.

In urban areas, trees improve the quality of life by providing shade, reducing noise pollution, and enhancing aesthetic appeal. They also have a positive impact on human health, with studies showing that exposure to green spaces can reduce stress levels and improve overall well-being.

Overall, trees are essential components of our ecosystems, and their preservation and conservation are paramount for the health and sustainability of our planet.

Yes, Terry, soon you will talk...
Mmm... Ma.. Mam..
Mother
Terry

Mama... I am playing
Okay, now you will study
Terry
Mother

Don't just play, there is another storm after Rainbows Remember!!
I will just come before sunset; the Rainbow is here It's just some hours!!
Mother
Terry

I forbade Terry to go!! Seems, the storm is coming!! Storm after Rainbows
Mother

Ohh!! GOD!!
I am Dying, Give
me Easy Death!!
My last ever
moments on
Earth
Mother

Mama!!! Where are you!! This can not be True!My mother can not Die!!
Terry

A few days Later...
Whatever Happened, just I need to forget & move on my life now!!
Terry

Hey, Terry
Do you remember your mother?
Why not?
Can you share any Memory with my mother?
When did you see her last?
Terry

Many years ago....
Hey, Merry Why so Happy?
I will soon have a Son in this lonely Life... He will be my support!
Mother

Hey, Terry
Let me share a
story of your
Late Beloved
mother!
Really!!
I would love
to hear it from
you!!
I miss her
a lot
Terry

Why are you so Happy today?
Many years ago.....
I have my Son in my Womb!! He will soon come to this World to live!
Mother

Why are you crying now!?
Don't Worry All will be OK
I am missing my Mother a lot now!!
Terry

Ohh, no!!
It's Drizzling
too much!
What's next?
Terry

Wow!!
It's the ...
Rainbows
Terry

Seems...it's the Storm... Storm after Rainbows?!
Terry

Ahh!! Mother told me earlier! This is the Destruction
Terry

I never should have Left my Mom alone in the storm!
I lost my mother in her loneliness
She needed me in the storm beside her!
Owhh..
I realize it now
After Rainbows there is—storm,
After Storms, there is,
SunRise!!
Terry

Kids Book Series from Big6 Publishing

Butterfly.png

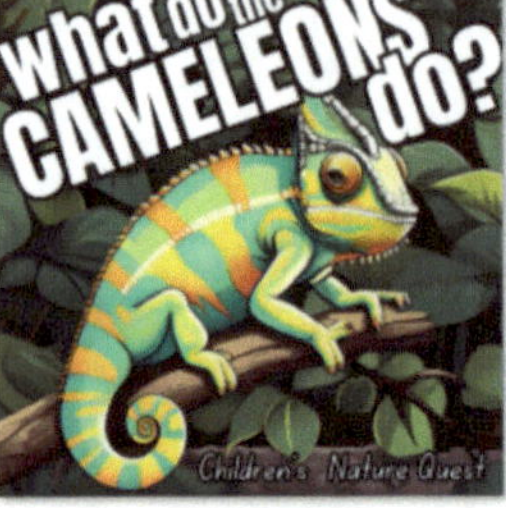

CAMELEON.png

how bees make honey.png

Life.png

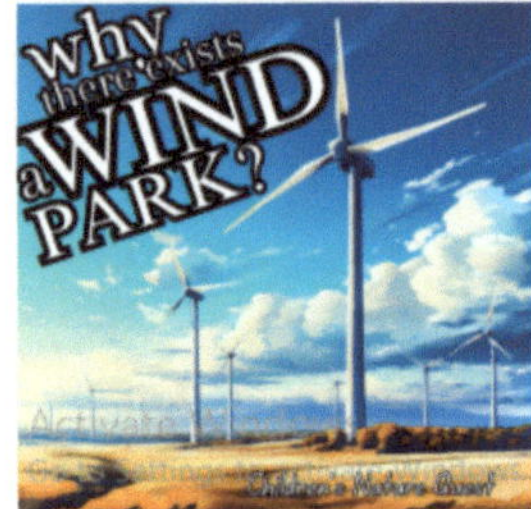

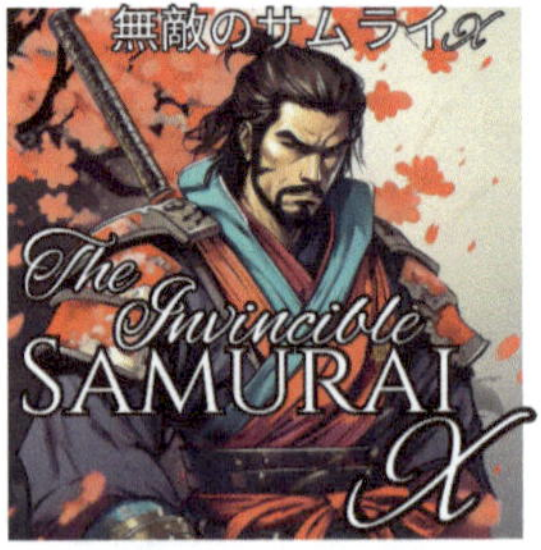

www.ingramcontent.com/pod-product-compliance
Lightning Source LLC
Chambersburg PA
CBHW041638110726
48005CB00002B/646